P9-CMY-144

Happy Jan &
Birthday, Jan &
God Bless You —
Love,
Missy

See Page 44

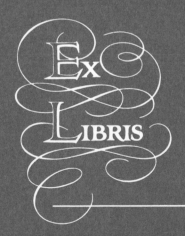

Ex Libris

April 17, 1983

Reflections of Love

Reflections of Love

Alice Joyce Davidson

Guideposts
CARMEL • NEW YORK 10512

Scripture quotations are from the King James Version of the Bible.

This Guideposts edition is published by
special arrangement with Fleming H. Revell Company.

Library of Congress Cataloging in Publication Data

Davidson, Alice Joyce.
Reflections of love.
1. Religious poetry, American. I. Title.
PS35564.A922R4   1982   811′.54   82-10211
ISBN 0-8007-1327-3

Dedicated to my husband, Marvin,
my partner in discovering
    the wonders of love,
    the fullness of life . . .
    the glory of God.

CONTENTS

FOREWORD

Helen Steiner Rice was a phenomenal woman whose talent touched the hearts of men, women, and children throughout the world. Her unique gift of blending words and wisdom, love and caring, faith and hope was always attributed by her as coming from the Divine Source. Helen proved a friend and mentor to Alice Joyce Davidson and, through her encouragement and close association, helped Alice develop her own poetic style. It is, truthfully, "in the tradition of Helen Steiner Rice."

Mrs. Davidson writes from the soul about feelings and experiences that are common to all of us. Love for friends, family, and country; joy in the beauty of nature with its changing seasons; feelings of grief, thanksgiving, and delight; and above all a deep, penetrating devotion to the Creator are some of the emotions shared in these poems.

As in her first volume, BECAUSE I LOVE YOU, Mrs. Davidson has written and illustrated this new work with her special artistic talents. We trust that her faithful followers and new readers alike will delight in each page of her "reflections" on everyday living.

The Publisher

From My Heart to Yours . . .

Words of friendship,
Words of love,
Words of praise
Of God above. . . .
Words of hope,
And faith and cheer
To share with someone
You hold dear.

With Love and Prayers,

Alice Joyce Davidson

Alice Joyce Davidson

. . . he is God in heaven above,
and in earth below.

Joshua 2:11

In Plain Sight

I see You, God, in fluffy clouds,
And in the sun's warm glow,
I see You in each drop of rain,
And every flake of snow,
I see You in each mountain peak,
And in the plains below.

I see You all around me
In every living thing,
In earthbound creatures great and small,
In birds that fly and sing,
I see You, God, in every bud
That blossoms in the spring.

I see You in each lacy leaf
That dances on a tree,
I see You, God, in everything
That You have caused to be—
And, when I look within myself,
I see You, God, in me!

Love Glow

Hallelujah!
I have felt it
   that tingle
   that glow
   that warmth
that inexplicable, electric energy
   that manifests itself
   in creativity
   and love!
Hallelujah, and praise the Lord!

**The Lord hath done great things for us;
whereof we are glad.**

Psalms 126:3

Creation

With one loving Hand,
Each atom was planned.

By one loving Mind,
The world was designed.

From one loving Heart,
Each soul got its start.

Behold, I am the Lord, the God
of all flesh: is there any thing too
hard for me?

Jeremiah 32:27

A Touch of Love

You can smell it in a flower,
You can see it in the sky,
You can feel it soft and gentle
As a summer breeze blows by—
   The touch of love is in the air!

You can show it with a smile,
You will know it when you pray,
It's a gift that's all around you
And inside you every day—
   God's touch of love is everywhere!

And we have known and believed the love
that God hath to us. God is love; and he that
dwelleth in love dwelleth in God, and God in him.

1 John 4:16

First Step

To begin,
  God, give me courage
    to begin.
Fill me with Your spirit,
  let me feel You
    deep within.
Give me dash and daring,
  confidence
    and heart
To take that first small step, God,
  to make
    a humble start!

The Lord is my strength and my shield;
my heart trusted in him, and I am helped. . . .

Psalms 28:7

Make Me a Channel, Lord!

Let me be a channel, Lord,
Through which Your love can flow.
Where I find darkness, let me bring
A warm and hopeful glow.
Help me, Lord, bring faith and trust
Where I find misbelief,
And let me wipe the tears that come
With sorrow, hurt, and grief.
Help me find the way, Lord,
To find new channels, too,
Through which Your love can flow until
The world is one with You!

**The fruit of the righteous is a tree of life;
and he that winneth souls is wise.**

Proverbs 11:30

When You Find Love

When you find love,
every sunrise
is more hopeful,
every day
is more fulfilling,
every sunset
is more beautiful.

When you find love,
God's wonders
are more wonderful,
and His promises
are more precious
and more real
than ever before!

No man hath seen God at any time.
If we love one another, God dwelleth
in us, and his love is perfected in us.

1 John 4:12

My Father's Home

No matter where I travel,
No matter where I roam,
I'm in my Father's kingdom,
So everywhere is "home."

My ceiling's made of fluffy clouds
Afloat in skies of blue,
My carpet's woven out of grass
And flowers fresh with dew.

My walls are made of mountains
And woods of stately trees,
My home is warmed by sunshine,
And in summer, cooled by breeze.

For joy and entertainment,
I have a constant show—
Songbirds singing, sunbeams dancing,
Dawn and dusk aglow.

And when my earthly days are done,
And I no longer roam,
I'll still be in His kingdom—
I'll be in my Father's home!

The earth is the Lord's,
and the fulness thereof; the world,
and they that dwell therein.

Psalms 24:1

Certainties

Thank You, God, for things to count on—
Steadfast things through all of time,
Knowing that You made the heavens,
Knowing that the sun will shine.

Thank You, God for making mountains,
Fertile valleys, streams and seas,
For love, for life that's everlasting—
Thank You, God, for certainties!

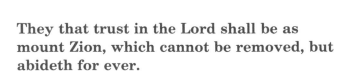

**They that trust in the Lord shall be as
mount Zion, which cannot be removed, but
abideth for ever.**

Psalms 125:1

God Believes in You

God endowed each one of us
With endless growing power.
Even when we fail, He knows
We'll try again another hour . . .
So never be discouraged,
Believe in all you do,
And keep on reaching higher
For God believes in you!

For the Lord shall be thy confidence. . . .

Proverbs 3:26

Loving Gentle,
Loving Strong

Lord, teach me to love gentle,
Give my heart a tender touch,
Help me show the warmth I feel
To those I love so much. . . .

Lord, teach me to love strong and firm,
To guide, to understand,
To be patient and forgiving,
To reach out a helping hand. . . .

Lord, teach me how to practice
All the many aspects of
The gift of gifts You gave us—
The precious gift of love!

But whoso keepeth his word, in him verily
is the love of God perfected: hereby know we
that we are in him.

1 John 2:5

26

Today

A mellow glow illumines the sky
   changing the moon to a silver sliver
      fading, as the darkness fades,
         into a pink-tinged sky.

Dawn comes.
   Today arrives
      greeted by the chattering of birds—
         a song that fills my heart with hope.

I breathe deeply of this new day
   grateful for the chance it brings
      to feel the love that flows around me—
to show the love that glows within me!

. . . when I awake, I am still with thee.

Psalms 139:18

America

Planning, forming, changing, growing,
Searching, finding, testing, knowing . . .
  MY COUNTRY 'TIS OF THEE,

Laughing, loving, praising, caring,
Playing, singing, dancing, sharing . . .
  SWEET LAND OF LIBERTY, OF THEE I SING,

Guarding, holding, shielding, fighting,
Grieving, aching, bleeding, righting . . .
  LAND WHERE MY FATHERS DIED,

Sailing, landing, hoping, praying,
Sowing, reaping, building, staying . . .
  LAND OF THE PILGRIMS' PRIDE

Working, making, taking, giving,
Speaking, hearing, choosing, living . . .
  FROM EVERY MOUNTAIN SIDE, LET FREEDOM RING!

**Blessed is the nation whose God is the Lord;
and the people whom he hath chosen . . . .**

Psalms 33:12

Growing Closer

We're doing it, Lord!
   We're getting there slowly.
      We're living a much better life,
Though You'd never tell
   from the headlines You read
      that scream about troubles and strife.

But read all of the pages,
   and in them You'll find
      a goodly abundance of
Stories of brotherhood,
   peace-seeking nations,
      charity, goodness, and love!

Day after day,
   in both big ways and small ways,
      the message You gave us gets through.
We're doing it, Lord!
   We're getting much better.
      We keep growing closer to You!

But the path of the just is as the shining light, that shineth more and more unto the perfect day.

Proverbs 4:18

Like as a father pitieth his children,
so the Lord pitieth them that fear him.

Psalms 103:13

Perfect Love

God's love is like a parent's love—
A love of pure perfection,
Of giving and forgiving,
Of caring and protection.

And like a loving parent,
God is always very near
To share a dream, a plan, a scheme,
To lend a listening ear.

He gives His children good advice,
And then He lets them go
To travel all life's hills and dales,
To learn to love . . . and grow.

He fills their world with wondrous gifts
Created with affection
For God's love is like a parent's love—
A love of pure perfection!

"O Give Thanks"

For the greatest wonders ever known,
Give thanks to God, and God alone,
  Whose love endures forever!

For heaven, earth, for day and night,
For sunshine, and for stars so bright,
For watching over with His might,
Give thanks to God, for in His light,
  Our love endures forever!

O give thanks unto the Lord; for he is good:
for his mercy endureth for ever.

Psalms 136:1

Well of Love

From faith's own Source,
we draw faith.

From hope's own Source,
we draw hope.

From love's own Source,
we draw love.

From life's own Source,
we draw life.

His well is endless, bottomless, infinite!

**Therefore with joy shall ye draw water
out of the wells of salvation.**

Isaiah 12:3

Day of Wonder, Day of Peace

Sabbath is a day of wonder
And of glad elation
When we review the miracle
Of six days of creation. . . .

Sabbath is a day of rest,
A day to slow our pace,
A day to look within ourselves
And find a quiet place. . . .

Sabbath is a day of peace,
A day for seeking good,
A day when friends and strangers
Join their hands in brotherhood!

**And God blessed the seventh day,
and sanctified it. . . .**

Genesis 2:3

The Good Shepherd

The Lord is my shepherd,
He shows me the way
To everything wonderful
Day after day . . .
He guides me and keeps me
From all kinds of harms,
And always He holds me
Within loving arms!

The Lord is my shepherd; I shall not want.

Psalms 23:1

A Leaf of Life

Dear Heavenly Gardener,
let me be a leaf
on Your tree of life.

In the sunshine of love,
let me grow,
and when winds blow,
let me bend.
Let me offer shelter
from the rain,
and shade to all
who rest below.

Let me be a leaf
on Your tree of life,
and when the seasons
come and go
and autumn brings
its sweet release,
let me gently fly the winds
and come to rest with You
in peace.

. . . whoso trusteth in the Lord,
happy is he.

Proverbs 16:20

36

Dawn to Dusk

At the start of the day
Take a moment to say
A greeting to God with a prayer,
Let your thoughts fill with love
As you praise Him above
For His Fatherly ways and His care. . . .

Then all through the hours,
Through sunshine and showers,
Through smiles, as well as through tears,
In all that you do
He will stay close to you
Doubling joys and dissolving your fears. . . .

And, when the day's through
And you stop and review
Each blessing and every event,
Thank God with a prayer
For His love and His care,
And your day will end wonderfully spent!

**From the rising of the sun unto the going down
of the same the Lord's name is to be praised.**

Psalms 113:3

To Mother

Yes, God is real to me.
   I see Him
      in your smile.
   I feel Him
      in your gentle ways.
   I know Him
      through the beauty
      of your soul.
Bless you!

Her children arise up, and call her blessed. . . .

Proverbs 31:28

As You Think

The mind is a wonderful
powerful thing;
What you imagine,
is what life will bring;
So, don't dwell on trouble,
misfortune or fear,
But how you can change them,
and they'll disappear . . .
Think positive thoughts
then watch as life brings
The best of God's blessings
and happiest things!

For as he thinketh in his heart, so is he. . . .

Proverbs 23:7

Days of Love

There are days of laughter,
   days of cheer,
   days of hope,
   and days of fear . . .
     and all of these are days of love.
There are days of learning,
   days of growing,
   days of tumult,
   and days of knowing . . .
     and all of these are days of love.

For every day
   on earth and heaven
Has been a day that
   God has given . . .
     all our days are gifts of love!

**Delight thyself also in the Lord; and he shall
give thee the desires of thine heart.**

Psalms 37:4

Possibilities

The more faith you have,
The more you believe,
The more goals you set,
The more you'll achieve . . .
So reach for the stars,
Pick a mountain to climb,
Dare to think big,
And give yourself time . . .
And, remember no matter
How futile things seem,
With faith, there is no
Impossible dream!

. . . for with God all things are possible.

Mark 10:27

. . . for the Lord thy God is with thee
whithersoever thou goest.

Joshua 1:9

God Is There With You

From dawn to dusk each waking day,
At worship, home, at work, or play,
God is there with you.

As you worship and you share
A meditation and a prayer,
God is there with you.

And, when your home, from floor to ceiling,
Fills with every tender feeling,
God is there with you.

And with each growing step you take,
Each contribution that you make,
God is there with you.

Through times for fun, and times of laughter,
Through memories that linger after,
God is there with you.

And when dark shadows fall in life,
When troubles come, through times of strife,
God is there with you.

Through every joy, through every tear,
Through every season of the year,
Always hold this gospel near—
God is there with you!

Hugs

There are hugs that say, "I like you
And I hold our friendship dear."
There are hugs that say, "Good going,
You deserve a great big cheer!"

There are hugs that say, "Goodbye, good luck
In all that lies ahead."
There are hugs that say, "I love you,"
When no other words are said.

There are hugs that soothe and say to us
"You're free from cares and harms"—
The kind of hug we feel when God
Holds us within His arms!

Be kindly affectioned one to another. . . .

Romans 12:10

44

Birthday Bouquet

I have a special yearning
As my birthday comes this year.
I don't relish hothouse orchids,
Or long-stemmed roses, Dear.
What I'd really like from you
Is just a country ride.
We'll find a big, old friendly tree
And sit down side by side
Among buttercups, pink clover,
Phlox, and wild daisies, too—
God made a sweet bouquet for me
I'd love to share with you!

. . . the earth is full of the goodness
of the Lord.

Psalms 33:5

Thanks Giving

For changing seasons, night and day,
We thank You
For Your forgiving, loving way,
We thank You,
For Your protection and Your care,
For all the wisdom that You share,
For all Your blessings everywhere,
We thank You.

**Let the heaven and earth praise him,
the seas, and every thing that moveth
therein.**

Psalms 69:34

The Ways of Love

Dear Lord,
Take my hand and hold it tight.
Guide me with Your golden light.
Let me learn humility.
Help me know tranquility.
Teach me how to work for good,
For peace on earth and brotherhood.
Show me all the ways of love
Fill my life with days of love!

A faithful man shall abound with blessings. . . .

Proverbs 28:20

Add Your Love to My Love

Lord, one I love is hurting,
soul-sick, heartsick,
sinking into the
quicksand of depression.

Try as I may,
I cannot reach,
cannot penetrate
the cold, cold, cold
hard shell.

Help me, Lord,
add Your love to my love.
Together we can lift,
together we can heal!

. . . perfect love casteth out fear. . . .

1 John 4:18

To Whom Our Praise Is Due

Praise the Lord for sunshine,
Praise the Lord for rain,
Praise the Lord for pleasure,
Praise the Lord for pain,
Praise the Lord for lessons learned
Through every joy and sorrow,
Praise the Lord for days gone by,
And for each new tomorrow!

O Lord, our Lord, how excellent is thy name in all the earth! who hast set thy glory above the heavens.

Psalms 8:1

Legacy

My days on earth are numbered,
So, dear God, with each new dawn,
Let me gather treasures
To leave when I've "gone on."

Help me fill a storehouse
With valuables like these—
Golden chains of friendship,
And crystal memories . . .

Give me pearls of wisdom,
A silver goblet of
The sweetest nectar ever—
The nectar of true love . . .

Fill my coffer, too, with smiles
That sparkle like the sun
(I'll purchase them with kindnesses
And thoughtful deeds I've done).

When my numbered days are finished
And, dear God, You beckon me,
Let me leave behind these treasures—
This living legacy!

. . . for the Lord preserveth the faithful,
and plentifully rewardeth the proud
doer.

Psalms 31:23

Love Song

When shall I hear You, Loving Lord,
When shall I hear You speak?
When I meditate in silence
By a slowly running creek!

When shall I hear Your music, Lord,
Each pure and measured note?
When a happy tune is rising
From a songbird's golden throat!

When shall I hear Your concert, Lord,
When shall the music play?
When brotherhood and love abound
And peace is here to stay!

When shall I hear Your lyrics, Lord,
Those words of faith and love?
When I pray to You sincerely—
When I'm One with You above!

... the prayer of the upright is his delight.

Proverbs 15:8

Let There Be Light!

What you see depends on you—
Depends upon your point of view.
If pessimism and despair
Have permeated everywhere,
If all you see is hatred churning,
A world that's filled with lust and yearning—
Let God turn on a light!

Close your eyes and say a prayer,
Put your problems in God's care.
He'll dispell the dark and gloom,
Your feelings of impending doom,
As He turns on a light.

For what you see depends on you—
Depends upon your point of view;
So set your goals and visions high
And if a dark cloud fills your sky—
Let God turn on a light!

Let not your heart be troubled. . . .

John 14:1

Finding Peace

Where does the search for peace begin?
Where can we make a start?
By looking first within ourselves,
Within our souls and hearts,
For You're the source of peace, dear Lord,
And if we follow You,
We will be led to lasting peace,
A peace profound and true!

The Lord bless thee, and keep thee:
The Lord make his face shine upon thee,
    and be gracious unto thee:
The Lord lift up his countenance upon thee,
    and give thee peace.

Numbers 6:24–26

Affirmation

Before the creation of man,
Before the creation of life,
Before the creation of the stars,
Before the creation of the first atom,
    There was the Creator.
        God was.
        God is.
        God always shall be for ever and ever.

**In the beginning God created
the heaven and the earth.**

Genesis 1:1

God Lives

In the heart
of a believer
God lives.
Through loving deeds and caring ways,
through joy-filled days and songs of praise,
He lives.

And in the heart
of a nonbeliever
waiting patiently, lovingly
for the time when He is called to be,
God lives!

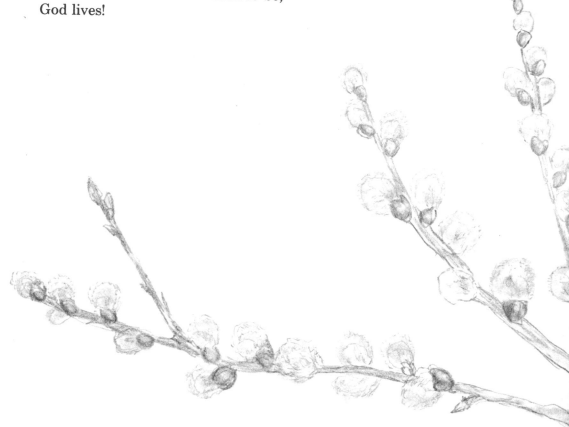

... blessed are they that have not seen,
and yet have believed.

John 20:29

Growing in Grace

My eyes
are growing dimmer,
yet I see more than I used to see.

My ears
are hearing less, and yet
I listen more perceptively.

Now some folks
will say I'm aging,
growing older, come what may,
but to me,
I'm just plain growing—
growing more in grace each day!

**With long life will I satisfy him,
and shew him my salvation.**

Psalms 91:16

Thy wife shall be as a fruitful vine by
the sides of thine house: thy children like
olive plants round about thy table.

Psalms 128:3

Family Tree

In the center of life's garden
A mother gently sows
A special seed, a seed of love
That sprouts, then grows and grows . . .
From day to day, from year to year,
She nurtures it with care,
Yet, understanding of its needs,
She gives it room and air . . .
Through winter, and through summer,
Through sun and rain filled hours,
The seedling reaches upward,
It branches, and it flowers . . .
In the center of life's garden
Grows a thing of majesty,
Rooted well with mother's love—
A blessed family tree!

My Friend

I have a Friend
who sees me
at my ugliest—
hateful, spiteful, boastful,
sinful—
but He forgives me!

. . . and because He forgives me
I can be beautiful!

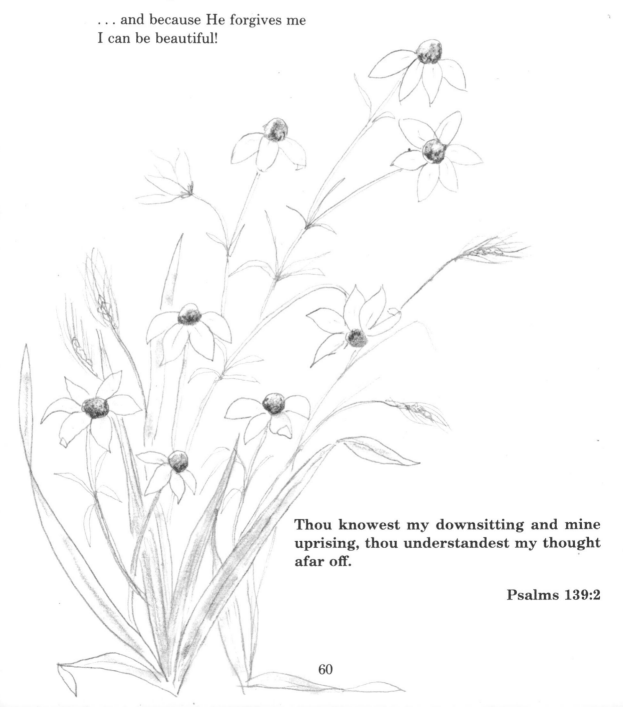

**Thou knowest my downsitting and mine
uprising, thou understandest my thought
afar off.**

Psalms 139:2

A Pact

Through my mouth,
Your words can flow,
Through my acts,
Your will can show,
Through Your love
My soul is blessed
With all that's true
And happiest!

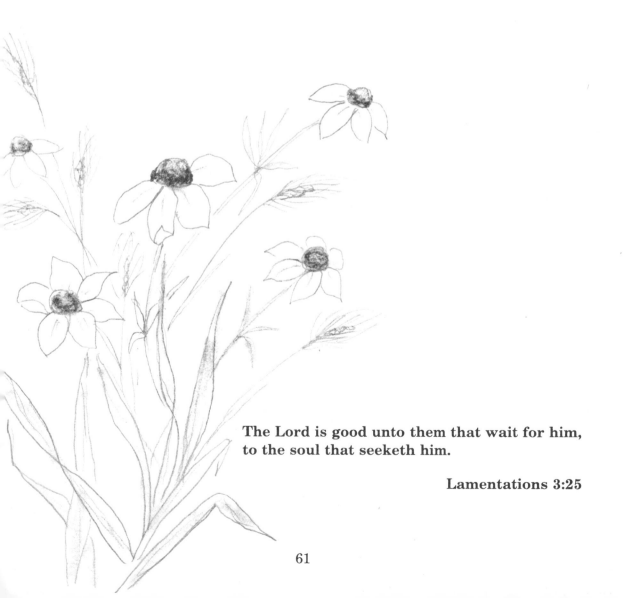

**The Lord is good unto them that wait for him,
to the soul that seeketh him.**

Lamentations 3:25

Seasons of Love

Love, like everything in life,
Has its many seasons—
A winter, springtime, summer
And autumn all its own.

Winter love is dormant
Softly sleeping in the snow
Waiting for a warming breeze
To stir it into life.

Springtime love is fragile
And precious as a swelling bud
Full of promises and dreams,
Of breathless beauty, too.

Summer love is wonderful—
A glowing, growing time
Full bloomed and brightly colored—
A sharing, caring time.

And autumn, golden autumn,
The harvest time of love
When fruits are picked and savored
And stored forevermore.

Let love be without dissimulation. . . .

Romans 12:9

Sing, Sing, Sing a Song!

My heart is filled with gladness,
My lips are filled with praise—
Oh, sing a song, Oh, sing a song
About His wondrous ways!

My life is filled with God's sweet gifts,
And love fills all my days—
Oh, sing a song, Oh, sing a song
About His wondrous ways!

Serve the Lord with gladness: come before his presence with singing.

Psalms 100:2

Sunbeam

Like a sunbeam
From above,
Choose a path
To light with love . . .
Bring a smile,
Lend an ear,
Share some words
Of faith and cheer . . .
Walk with God,
Have sunshine ways,
And you'll be blessd
With happy days!

But the path of the just is as the shining light, that shineth more and more unto the perfect day.

Proverbs 4:18

Twin Circles

Love and faith
are twin circles.

They each begin with God;
and the more they are used
the more powerful
they grow . . .

and just like perfect circles,
they each
are never ending.

**But without faith it is impossible
to please him: for he that cometh to
God must believe that he is, and that
he is a rewarder of them that diligently
seek him.**

Hebrews 11:6

Showers of Blessings

As I give thanks,
I keep finding more
Wonderful things
To be thankful for . . .
So, thank You, dear God,
For Your gifts from above,
The showers of blessings
You send with Your love!

It is a good thing to give thanks unto the Lord. . . .

Psalms 92:1

Sweet Memories

The growing-up-together days,
The sunshine, and bad-weather days,
The holidays, the times of cheer,
The friendly chats, a listening ear,
The fun that comes from giving, sharing,
The warmth, and all the love and caring—
The sweetest family memories
Are made of special things like these!

. . . thou shalt rejoice, thou, and
thine household.

Deuteronomy 14:26

A Question

A child asked a wise man,
"Does my doggie have a soul?
Will she be rewarded
If heaven is her goal?"

The wise man paused a moment,
Then he shook his head,
"I don't know the answer
For the Bible never said
Anything about a dog
As part of God's great plan
When He breathed eternal life
Into the soul of man."

"But my doggie was very good,
She took good care of me,
She loved so hard, I know that she
Deserves eternity."

The wise man stroked his beard and said,
"If what you say is true,
Then when you get to heaven,
You'll find your dog there, too!"

. . . the Lord will give grace and glory:
no good thing will he withhold from them
that walk uprightly.

Psalms 84:11

A Child's Meditation

I may be small
But I can be
As tall as any
Redwood tree
　　When You're within my heart!

My faith is simple
Pure and true.
There's nothing, Lord,
That I can't do
　　When You're within my heart!

**Be ye therefore followers of God,
as dear children.**

Ephesians 5:1

Blessed is the man that trusteth in the Lord, and whose hope the Lord is.

Jeremiah 17:7

Bright Hope

When it's grey and cloudy
And the skies just pour and pour,
Have you ever doubted
That the sun would shine once more?

After being frozen
By a winter's frost and snow,
Have you ever questioned
Whether springtime buds would grow?

Sometimes life brings cloudy skies,
And cold and wintry days—
These, too, will melt away beneath
Hope's bright and warming rays!

Holiday Prayer

Let us pray
this holy day
with feeling—
Not with sullen spirit
nor a mood of levity
reciting idle chatter
or mere frivolity—
But let us pray
this holy day
with feeling—
Feeling love
that's deep and true
for each other
and for You!

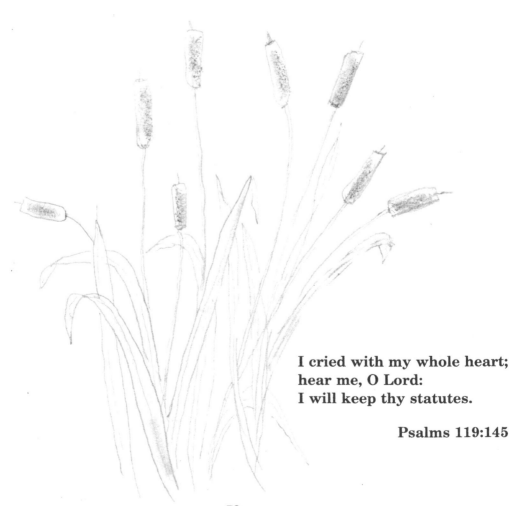

I cried with my whole heart;
hear me, O Lord:
I will keep thy statutes.

Psalms 119:145

Countless Blessings

Grey skies give way to skies of blue,
The wind has lost its sting,
As gently, ever gently,
Nature ushers in the spring.

The morning brings a robin's song,
The noon, a warming sun,
And sunset shows the silhouette
Of budding that's begun.

Our hearts are overcome with joy,
Our spirits fill with cheer,
As the miracle of springtime
And rebirth once more is here.

And as we think of all God's gifts
And blessings that are ours,
We find that they're as countless
As His lovely springtime flowers!

This is the Lord's doing; it is
marvellous in our eyes.

Psalms 118:23

little prayer

Lord,
give us vision
to see a little further . . .
give us strength
to try a little harder . . .
give us faith
to reach a little higher,
to become a little better . . .
and then a little more!

. . . teach them the good way
wherein they should walk . . . .

1 Kings 8:36

Compassion

I try to be good,
But try as I would,
Sometimes I slip and I fall . . .
But God looks inside,
And He knows that I tried,
And forgives my mistakes one and all!

The Lord is gracious, and full of compassion; slow to anger, and of great mercy.

Psalms 145:8

Supreme Power

Though languages divide us,
though customs divide us,
though oceans divide us,
   in our hearts,
   in our minds,
   in our souls,
     we are one.

The One God unites us!

For God is the King of all the earth. . . .

Psalms 47:7

When You Have Faith

Days are filled with hopeful hours
And rainbows always follow showers,
    When you have faith!

There's no problem you can't face,
No sorrows that you can't erase,
    When you have faith!

Your little worries all will cease,
And you'll be filled with inner peace,
    When you have faith!

There's nothing that you cannot do,
No favorite dream that can't come true,
No mountain is too high for you,
    When you have faith!

**But they that wait upon the Lord
shall renew their strength. . . .**

Isaiah 40:31

New Life

Mother Nature tiptoes in
On cold and barren earth,
And, with a warm and tender touch,
She calls new life to birth . . .

With a kiss of sunlight,
She coaxes sap to flow,
And crocuses to push their blooms
Through slowly melting snow . . .

She takes her springtime palette,
And, with strokes so sure and true,
She colors brown grass green once more,
And paints the heavens blue . . .

Songbirds bid her springtime call
To fly back home, and then
Join the endless cycle
To renew life once again . . .

And, as she calls new life to birth,
As only Nature can,
She reminds us of the promise
Of God's Eternal Plan.

**And this is the promise that he hath
promised us, even eternal life.**

1 John 2:25

Bedtime Question

Did I take time to listen
To a troubled heart today?
Did I take time to smile
As a stranger came my way?
Did I take time to share a load,
To lighten someone's cares?
Did I take time to go to God
In thankful thought and prayers?
Did I take time today to love?
Did I take time to give?
Did I take time to grow today?
Did I take time to live?

My little children, let us not love
in word, neither in tongue; but in
deed and in truth.

1 John 3:18

Ebb of Time

Days follow days, and years follow years
As time goes slipping by . . .
We can't hold back the ebb of time
No matter how we try . . .
But, if you live life fully
And joyfully, you'll find
That as long as you're still growing,
Age is just a state of mind . . .
So never give up reaching
For a goal, however bold,
And never give up dreaming,
And you never will grow "old"!

Yea, the Lord shall give that
which is good. . . .

Psalms 85:12

Uninvited

Every so often
it sneaks in
uninvited.

Conquering, crushing,
clouding the mind,
like a window shade
closing out the sunlight,
a black mood sets in
filling the spirit
with sadness—
leaving no room for joy.

And overpowered by the weight,
with knees upon the ground,
a whispered prayer escapes—

And God turns on a light.

**For thou wilt light my candle:
the Lord my God will enlighten
my darkness.**

Psalms 18:28

Stepping-Stone

When you travel down life's highway
With an extra heavy load,
When you come upon a byway
That's a deeply pitted road,
Don't hesitate to walk on through,
Let faith become a stepping-stone,
Remember, God is there with you—
You never travel all alone!

. . . be not dismayed; for I am thy God:
I will strengthen thee. . . .

Isaiah 41:10

One Song Is Sung

Your people, God, are scattered.
We each have our own tongue,
But from every corner of the earth
One song of praise is sung:
    We praise You for Your wonders—
    The sunshine and the storm,
    We praise You for the miracles
    Which You alone perform.

We pray in many languages,
Your people are far-flung,
But in unity and harmony,
One song of hope is sung:
    Father, bind us closer
    To find a common good
    So we may work together
    In peace and brotherhood!

Peace be to the brethren, and love with faith. . . .

Ephesians 6:23

The Beach of Time

Standing on a beach we see
  a small part of the ocean,
    the vast and mighty ocean
      that stretches on and on.

It's difficult to comprehend
  the mysteries it holds,
    the splendor and the rhythm
      of the tide . . . of dusk and dawn.

Standing on the beach of time
  how can we understand
    the splendor and the mystery
      of life . . . and all beyond?

**The Lord on high is mightier than the noise
of many waters, yea, than the mighty waves
of the sea.**

Psalms 93:4

Proposal

Come
dream along
with me.

Share
my thoughts
my wants
my pillow
my needs.

Come
grow along
with me.

Care
with me
dare
with me
share
life's smiles and trials
with me.

Come
dream along
with me.

My beloved spake, and said unto me,
Rise up, my love, my fair one, and come away.

Song of Solomon 2:10

Wedding Prayer

Dear Lord,
Thank You for giving us
Your supreme gift of love.
Thank You for giving us
each other.
Thank You for giving us
the wonderful adventure
of marriage.

Guide us through
the pathways of life.
If we falter,
give us faith.
If we stumble,
lift us up.

Give us strength
to climb the steepest slopes
and reach the highest peaks.
Give us fortitude
to ride the biggest waves
and withstand the tides of time.

In the sunshine of Your love
let us discover new ways
of growing together,
of growing individually . . .
of growing closer, Lord, to You!

. . . and they twain shall be one. . . .

Matthew 19:5

Cast Your Vote

When you don't want to go along
With something that you know is wrong,
  say NO!
Don't be ruled by any crowd,
Don't be afraid to shout out loud
  NO!
True, it's just a little word,
But it has power when it's heard,
So cast your vote, don't ever sway,
Keep on walking in God's way,
Don't ever hesitate to say
  NO!

**Enter not into the path of the wicked, and go not
the way of evil men.**

Proverbs 4:14

A Forever Friend

Through good times,
And through bad times,
Through glad times,
And through sad times,
   A friend is always there!

Through up times,
And through down times,
Through smile times,
And through frown times,
   A friend will always care!

A friend loveth at all times. . . .

Proverbs 17:17

But thou, O Lord, shalt endure for ever;
and thy remembrance unto all generations.

Psalms 102:12

Grandmother's Gift

Sweet little baby
Asleep in my arms
You've stolen my heart
With your dearness and charms.

Precious one, precious one,
How can I start
Repaying the joy
That you've brought to my heart?

For this gift that you gave me,
I'll give in return
A lesson to help you
Throughout life's sojourn.

Look for the sunshine,
Face life with a smile,
Always have hope
And a dream that's worthwhile.

Reach for the stars,
Know all kinds of love,
And never lose faith
In our Father above!

Within Our Choosing

God gave to each of us
the wonderful power
to choose.

Let us choose good,
    not evil;
let us choose peace,
    not war;
let us choose love,
    not hate;
let us choose oneness
with each other
    and with God!

**Mercy unto you, and peace, and love,
be multiplied.**

Jude 2

Entreaty

Open
my
eyes, Lord,
the better to serve You . . .
Open
my
mind, Lord,
the better to know You . . .
Open
my
arms, Lord,
the better to hold You . . .
Open
my
heart, Lord,
the better to love You!

For thy loving kindness is before mine eyes. . . .

Psalms 26:3

Grief

Heavy, heavy, heavy
My heart is heavy, Lord,
One I loved and cherished
Just went to her reward,
And I feel so very selfish
To want her near me when
She was eagerly awaiting
To be with You again;
So, I'll hold my tears and grief inside
And say this two-part prayer—
First of all, please keep her, Lord,
Within Your loving care,
And then, I want to thank You, Lord,
For especially blessing me
With days I'll cherish always
In loving memory!

**Blessed are they that mourn:
for they shall be comforted.**

Matthew 5:4

Everlasting Candle

The candle of faith
is an everlasting light . . .
a wick of belief
burning bright
in an endless reservoir
of love.

I am come a light into the world, that
whosoever believeth on me should
not abide in darkness.

John 12:46

Alighting

Love
flies in
on the wings
of a butterfly.
Delicate
yet strong
and ever so beautiful!

My beloved is mine, and I am his. . . .

Song of Solomon 2:16

Quiet Place

I have a quiet place
where I can go to rest
from tension, cares, and trials,
from turmoil and daily tests.

A quiet place within
where I can be
alone with me . . .
alone with Thee!

**Thou art my hiding place and my shield;
I hope in thy word.**

Psalms 119:114

Working for Peace

Dear Lord, I've just been thinking
How patient You must be
To hear the prayers Your children pray
In mock sincerity . . .
We pray that You will grant us
Your most precious gift of peace,
We pray that You will intercede
And cause all strife to cease;
But when our prayers are finished,
What do we really do
To work for peace among ourselves
To help our prayers come true?

Lord, grant to us the courage
And make us wise and strong
To use the precious tools of peace
Which we've had all along—
The tools of understanding,
Of charity and sharing,
Of being open-minded,
And more loving and more caring,
So we may band together
Working for the common good,
And grant ourselves the precious gifts
Of peace and brotherhood!

**Let us therefore follow after
the things which make for peace. . . .**

Romans 14:19

Mothers Are Love

Mothers are created
  as reflections
    of the Lord.

They give life,
  and they're life itself—
    they're love and love's reward!

**Thou sendest forth thy spirit,
they are created: and thou renewest
the face of the earth.**

Psalms 104:30

Lull-a-Baby

Hush dear baby, hush my sweet,
The Lord is by your side
Watching o'er you as the door
To Dreamland opens wide....
Hush, hush baby, hush my sweet,
Peace be with you, Dear,
When you sleep and when you wake
The Lord is always near.

**For he shall give his angels charge
over thee, to keep thee in all thy ways.**

Psalms 91:11

A Goal

Dear God,
give me a goal
impossible to reach
so that when I reach it,
I'll know that nothing
is impossible!

The desire accomplished is sweet to the soul. . . .

Proverbs 13:19

Partnership

A new day just began, Lord,
A brand new day has started,
And I'm prepared to meet it
Feeling good and hopeful hearted . . .

I'm ready for new challenges,
New vistas to explore,
And any opportunities
The day might hold in store . . .

There are problems to be answered,
Solutions to be found—
But the two of us together,
We can turn the world around!

**Commit thy way unto the Lord; trust
also in him; and he shall bring it to pass.**

Psalms 37:5

Love Power

It's love,
pure and simple love,
that can turn this world around.
Not, power, not might,
just love.

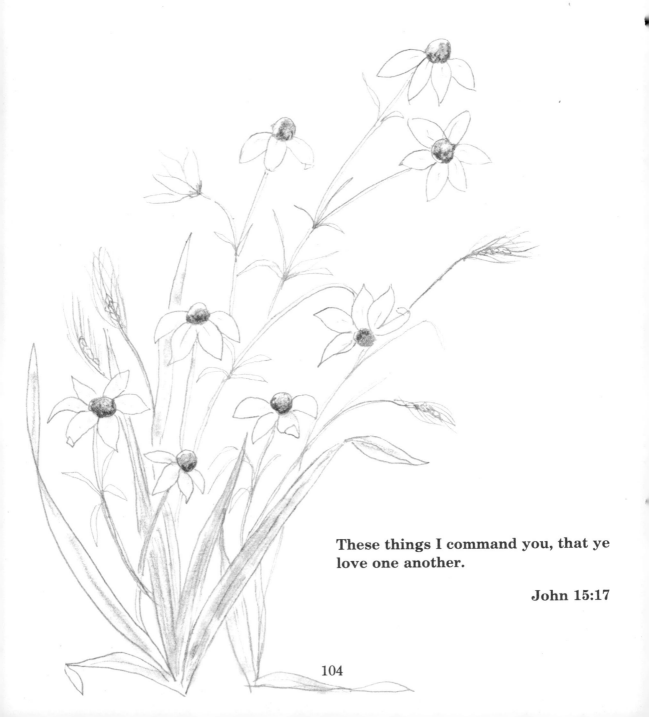

**These things I command you, that ye
love one another.**

John 15:17

Heaven's Gate

The Gateway of Heaven
is not made of gold
encrusting rare diamonds
and pearls.

The Gateway of Heaven
is made in the heart
out of faith, selfless deeds
and of love.

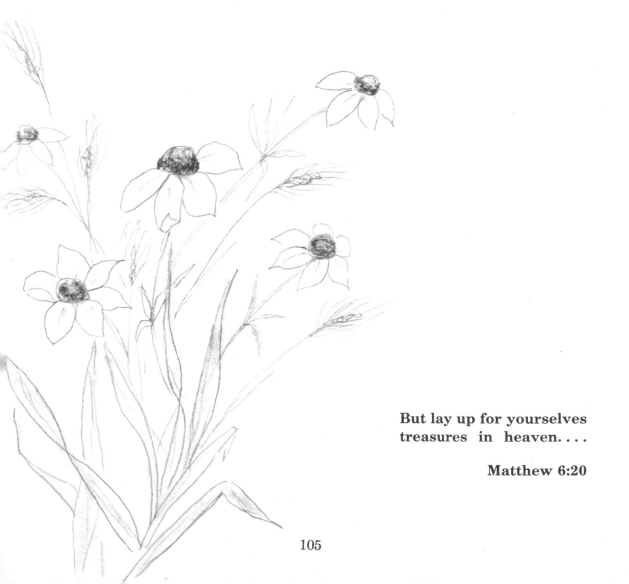

But lay up for yourselves
treasures in heaven. . . .

Matthew 6:20

Flower of the Field

In nature's world
every little flower
grows, blossoms,
and leaves its mark
on the earth which hosted it.

We, too, are part
of nature's world . . .
growing, blossoming,
leaving our mark.

. . . All flesh is grass,
and all the goodliness thereof
is as the flower of the field.

Isaiah 40:6

Autumn Ball

You're invited to an autumn ball,
The last fling of the year,
So dress up in your finest jewels,
Your gold and rubies, Dear . . .
We'll waltz to northern breezes
A-smiling and a-whirling
Waiting for the signal
To send our jewels a-twirling . . .
And when the ball is over
And we've had our autumn fling,
We'll take a little winter nap
Until the first of spring!

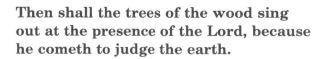

**Then shall the trees of the wood sing
out at the presence of the Lord, because
he cometh to judge the earth.**

1 Chronicles 16:33

Fathers

Fathers are for talking with,
For words that guide and cheer,
Fathers are for walking with,
For always being near,
Fathers are for caring,
For being strong, yet gentle,
Fathers are for sharing
When you're feeling sentimental,
Fathers are for standing by
Through every kind of strife—
Fathers are for giving faith
That lights your way through life!

For I know him, that he will command
his children and his household after him,
and they shall keep the way of the Lord. . . .

Genesis 18:19

Costly Treasure

Friendship is a treasure
Which anyone can buy,
But be prepared to pay a lot—
The purchase price is high . . .
It costs in time and patience,
And a wealth of selfless deeds,
In giving and forgiving,
And fulfilling special needs,
It costs in understanding,
In listening, and in caring,
It costs in sweet forbearance,
In loving, and in sharing . . .
Yes, friendship is a treasure,
And though the cost is high,
The more you pay, the more it's worth
As time goes passing by!

Two are better than one;
because they have a good reward
for their labour.

Ecclesiastes 4:9

Fellowship

I walked
into the chapel
a stranger.

I shared song,
prayers,
and feelings
with those
around me.

And when I walked out,
I was among friends!

For where two or three are gathered
together in my name, there I am in the
midst of them.

Matthew 18:20

Link of Faith

Life
is a chain
of events, experiences, and growth . . .
and faith
is the golden clasp
that links the chain of life
full circle
to God!

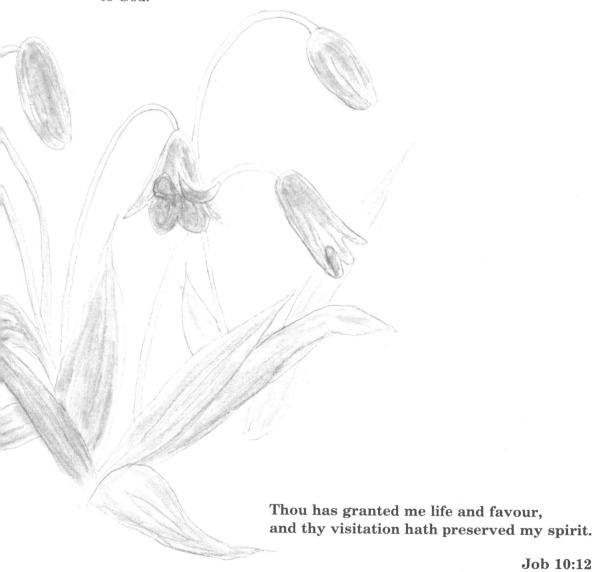

Thou has granted me life and favour,
and thy visitation hath preserved my spirit.

Job 10:12

Warm Snow

Three inches high,
   it hugs the ground,
     a blanket of new snow,
Reflecting back
   the sunshine
     in a bright and cheerful glow. . . .

"Three inches high!"
   the children yelp,
     their happy eyes aglow

As they make
   angel tracks upon
     a warm inviting snow.

. . . thou hast made summer and winter.

Psalms 74:17

Gifts! Gifts! Gifts!

Gifts, gifts, lovely gifts,
The best that money buys,
Box them, wrap them, pack them, stack them,
Watch the pile rise!

Gifts, gifts, lovely gifts!
Open up your eyes,
And see the greatest gift of all
Which money never buys.

Gifts, gifts, wondrous gifts!
All that you're dreaming of,
Each one is wrapped in sunshine
And tied with special love . . .

Gifts of faith and fortitude,
Of brotherhood, and love,
Gifts of comfort, hope, and peace
Are yours from God above!

. . . nor trust in uncertain riches,
but in the living God, who giveth us richly
all things to enjoy.

1 Timothy 6:17

This is the day which the Lord hath made. . . .

Psalms 118:24

This Is the Day

Second by second,
And minute by minute,
Today will have
Everything opportune in it—
New things to discover,
New roads to explore,
By the end of today,
I'll know more than before—
New things I can learn,
New things I can see,
For God made this day
Especially for ME!

A Merry Heart

Doom and gloom
Can fill a room
And leave a sickly feeling . . .
An upturned chin,
And happy grin
Is so much more appealing!

A merry heart doeth good like a medicine. . . .

Proverbs 17:22

Morning

"Wake-up, wake-up,"
   the birds are singing,
     "it's a lovely day.
Chirup, chirup, chirup,
  it's bringing
     lots of joy your way!"

. . . joy cometh in the morning.

Psalms 30:5

So teach us to number our days,
that we may apply our hearts unto wisdom.

Psalms 90:12

Resolution

A brand new year is here again,
It's time to make a date
To meet the Lord, to cleanse your soul,
To start a brand new slate!

Don't look back on yesterday,
It's over with and gone,
But put your best foot forward
And prepare to meet the dawn!

A brand new year is here again,
Let hope, and faith, and love
Shine from your heart the way God's love
Shines on you from above!

Insomnia

I tossed and turned with worry—
What will the morning bring?
The new day brought a headache,
And each eye its own dark ring!

I wish I had remembered
To take the Good Book out
And read the words to calm my fears
And chase away each doubt!

**Seek ye out of the book of the Lord,
and read. . . .**

Isaiah 34:16

Gift List

Sunshine, flowers,
Happy hours,
Rainbow skies
To follow showers,
A roof above,
Good things to eat,
A joyful deed,
New friends to meet,
Hugs and kisses
Filled with love—
All these are gifts
From God above!

**Blessed be the Lord, who daily loadeth us
with benefits. . . .**

Psalms 68:19

Remember Me?

You come to Me
on bended knee
whenever shadows fall . . .
but do you think to call on Me
when happy things surround you?

You feel quite free
to come to Me
for favors big and small . . .
but do you think to thank Me for
the miracles around you?

O give thanks unto the Lord:
call upon his name: make known his deeds
among the people.

Psalms 105:1

Loving Heart

Take my heart
and make it
Your dwelling place
so that everyone
I touch
will be touched also
by You!

. . . Be perfect, be of good comfort, be of one mind,
live in peace; and the God of love and peace
shall be with you.

2 Corinthians 13:11

I Am an American

I am as much a part of America
   as America is a part of me.

I am the voice of America,
   the molder of truths,
   the sieve which sifts
   rights from wrongs.

My being is the substance of America.
   I am the thinker, the maker,
   the tiller, the doer . . . the provider.

I am the soul of America,
   the creator of history,
   the giver and user of freedom and rights.

I am the product of the past,
   the seed for tomorrow.

I am America
and America is me!

. . . the nations shall bless themselves in him. . . .

Jeremiah 4:2

Mirror

In love
You gave us life, dear Lord,
and blessed us
with a soul . . .
Help us to use
these blessings,
with love
our common goal!

. . . Blessed is he that cometh in the
name of the Lord. . . .

Matthew 21:9

A Poet's Prayer

Guide my pen, Lord!

Together
we'll knock on the doors
to hearts
shedding light
where there is darkness,
giving hope
where there is despair.

We'll visit busy cities,
country towns,
and remote corners of the world
preaching the Fatherhood of God,
the brotherhood of man.
We'll shout oneness from mountain tops.

Take my hand, Lord!
Together
We'll light the world with love!

**. . . the Lord shall be unto thee
an everlasting light. . . .**

Isaiah 60:19